Silica to Quartz

Johanita Viljoen

Published by EBNI's POEMS & SCRIPTS, 2024.

SILICA TO QUARTZ

First edition. November 27, 2024.

ISBN: 979-8230529583

Written by Johanita Viljoen.

Table of Contents

Silica to Quartz

Whispers of Stone!

Johanita's Poems from the heart

With thanksgiving to my Heavenly Father Who guided and
kept met through the time of writing.

To my ever-half, family, friends, - you are the ones who always
motivated me!

Poet's Song

Grains of sand, rough, coarsely scattered,

silica transforms into polished stones, beautifully mattered!

Little pebbles now smooth and rounded, shaped by rain and water.

Precious quartz, crystals, polished like jewels for later!

Little letters, words, lines found,

still incoherent, searching, from the pen of a child unbound.

Poetic thoughts exposed, unfold, with time grow strong,

Little poems, surprising on the lips, a poet's amazing song!

Silica to Quartz
Whispers of Stone

Author: Johanita Viljoen
Cover Design and Illustrations: Johanita utilizing AI

Other Books by Author:
Hartspalmpies by Waterstroompies Deel 1; Malherbe Publishers
https://bit.ly/Hartspalmpies1
Hartspalmpies by Waterstroompies Deel 2; Malherbe Publishers
https://bit.ly/Hartspalmpies-2
By die Oewer; Malherbe Publishers
https://bit.ly/BydieOewer
Reënboog Lantern; Malherbe Publishers
https://bit.ly/reenbooglantern
Little Heart Palms by Stream Sides; Malherbe Publishers
https://bit.ly/LittleHeartPalms
River Side Under a Rainbow Lantern; Malherbe Published

O Reader, so special so dear!
Perhaps, in a corner, you sit today,
spirit broken, tears rolled, you sway.
A grain of sand, swept off, só confused,
struggling, searching, your heart suffered, bruised!
Many uncertainties weigh on your soul -
unexpected illness, violence, death a toll.
May poetic words ease your heart's silent plea -
heavenly comfort to help you be free!
To relax and smile through both joy and despair,
read Isaiah 43, find solace in prayer!
And may that tiny grain of silica becomes bright,
unfolding like quartz, bringing beauty and light!
Wishes from my heart,
Johanita

My Spacesuit

I purchased a brand-new spacesuit,
    my savings emptied, without dispute!
    My finger points towards the beautiful moon,
    to where I'll venture, oh, very soon!
    No more tedious routine to bear!
    Who wants to go to school every day? I declare...
    My suit is pristine white, incredibly unique,
    to match the rocket's thrilling wreak.
    I haven't told Mom yet, you see,
    afraid she'll worry, making a plea!
    She might never see her son again,
    as he whirls through space, on count of ten!
    The machine stands ready in the open field.
    In front of Grandpa's old mobile, fate is sealed!
    The homemade rocket stands firmly in place,
    bolted tight with tools from Dad's toolbox case.
    I'm grateful we live out here on the farm,
    where the rocket-engine won't cause much alarm!
    Unfortunately, Big Brother arrives at the launching site,
    stopping commotion before petrols ignite.
    In my white suit, with a flamy match in the hand,
    I yearned to travel to space, to the grand!
    But Big Brother, Dad, and Mom scolded me só,
    I'll have to wait till I'm grown, thén I'll give it a go!

Trivialities

Trivialities, -
    the greatest cause indeed,
    of mumbling, complaining!
    Só dissatisfied, with speed,
    unnecessary, indiscreet!
    With empty words to dance,
    just false notes, askance!
    No harmony or accord,
    only frowning, of some sort!
    And time slips away,
    with no happiness to stay.
    Completely lost in disarray!

Storm Rider

Restless, always busy, in constant motion,
here and there, seeking quietness, a silent notion!
A day has only twenty-four fleeting hours,
so much to do before sleep's calling powers.
While eyes closed, the brain works overtime,
planning tomorrow's schedule, secure and prime.
Daybreak quickly dawns, traffic becomes fierce,
various tasks in a stormy rush, what a pierce!
The dust devil of busy life, no respite is granted,
hardly time to eat a sandwich, totally frazzled!
What good to be hustled and perpetual bustled?
What is the race without a true goal in its tussle?
As towering man-made buildings rise ever high,
constructed with hammers and trowels, oh my!
Higher and larger skyscrapers erected,
for great wealth at stake, and riches projected!
The city's multitude tirelessly swarm,
in gale and haste, devoid of purpose's form!
By standing aside and observing the scene,
one grows weary, yearning for countryside serene!
Every forehead bears worried lines, certain gates left ajar,
anxiety and weariness evident, etched afar!
Rude and clumsy someone rushes by,
to swiftly obtain their own small piece, oh my!
They may pause briefly for a fleeting while,
but mostly, restless and forcefully, they'll compile.
No peace, no rest, thé chaotic human soul!

Will you ever find tranquil contentment, as a whole?

Humanity's Maelstrom

Churning waters
    deep abysses
    where-in darknesses will thrive
    no happy existence or good life!
    A tempestuous being
    cloaked in the haze of earthly living
    filled with worry and worldly stain
    never steadfast, nor in the right lane.
    Pleasure, excitement in worldly delight
    driven by desires, forsaking God's might
    bounded, entangled in a chain
    heavier the load in each existing pain.
    Oh, tempestuous being
    driven by wind, without seeing
    desires shortens life's abode
    seizes chances of an untroubled road!
    The Lord's Word, your only hope
    renewed, reborn, forever to cope
    for there is pure, life-giving water, supreme
    for those walking the Narrow Path, extreme!
    Plenty burdens in humanity's maelstrom
    but He leads a loved one out of each storm
    Jesus, the Way, the Truth, the Life
    to set the soul free from earthly strife!

Voice from the Woods

A voice from the woods, a voice of violence,
    a child, innocent and small, vanishing in silence!
    Searches launched, yet no one can tell
    of this little boy's bitter, harrowing hell.
    There's a voice that cries from the ominous wood,
    the child's frail body left right where they stood.
    A heartless creature, untouched by remorse,
    destroy and abandon this tiny soul, in bitter course.
    Injuries and cruel bruises marred the lovely child,
    lying amidst the leaves, will someone find him, in the wild?
    Abused and cold, pleading eyes wide open,
    no fault of his own, his face, deadly pale and broken.
    Cruelty of a disordered, heartless man,
    unleashing frustration on this fragile little lamb.
    Is it his voice that one hears calling out,

for help or revenge, for his innocent blood, so loud?

The Calling Voice

Frantic pursuit of the wind's fleeting gust!
    Where do you run, earthly child, in this hurried thrust?
    Do you truly seek, in perfect, pure, infinite delight?
    Beware, stay away from the root of all evil, a cunning fright!
    Where wealth and vanity falsely fuels your vein,
    what about the moth, the rust, a deceitful game!
    Satan himself shines in the midst of revelry's flame!
    Does your devious cup never fill, always the same?
    A released and pleasure-seeker, falling for the deceiver's aim!
    Few are those who seek the path of peace,
    towards grace, from earthly unease!
    Weary wanderers, longing for a renewed stance,
    with a genuine prayer, to forever enhance.
    Here I stand, your Father, not far away.
    Do you listen to My calling voice today?

Weep, speak, your case is secure as I hold you tight!
    Hear My voice, I am your Heavenly Father, there's light!
    Come to Me, I shall draw nearer, into your view.
    My child, I am gathering the harvest, to refresh and anew!
    My voice calls out, find peace, there is hope!
    Times are changing, signs taking a rapid slope.
    Once more, I call to you, remember I'm God
    I bought you dearly with My blood.

The Dark Sea

Oh, somber sea, a haunting sight,
   colossal force that engulfs the night.
   You carry all within your deep,
   a wealth of life, no shortage to keep!
   You rumble and roar, in a murky dense shroud,
   waves of terror, fierce and proud!
   Brave sailors sink beneath your might,
   in watery depths, their souls take flight.
   A foreboding mass of water vast,
   with tales of sorrow, haunting, steadfast.
   Yet, oh, dark sea, you captivate
   in surrounded beauty that hearts can sate,
   Your waters stretch, calm and serene,
   with seashells scattered, a tranquil scene!
   Enticing millions with glamor and lure,
   white-capped waves upon the shore as cure.
   Ice cream stalls with treats galore,
   laughter resonates, as feet explore.
   On the distant horizon, far and wide,
   you blend with sun and clouds beside,
   Passenger ships glide, smooth and daring,
   Fishing boats roam in sunlight glaring.
   Mysterious and ever-changing, you will remain,
   A fascination that none can or will disdain!

Seagulls and Fishes

Several seagulls fly low above the sea,
> where white waves brush, on seasand free.
> Transparent, clean, the water so clear,
> rippling over small, orange pebbles near.
> The winged creatures think there's a lovely feast!
> But clever little swimmers, aware of this beast!
> To snatch a fish is an art so rare,
> flying back and forth, they must beware.
> Fish swiftly bend their bodies and dive,
> deep into water, survival's strive!
> Dodge and swim, dodge and swim, almost caught...
> the birds' sharp claws, eagerly sought!
> Wildly, sleek bodies glide beneath the tide,
> soaring and diving, with grace they abide.
> A seagull scoops up the poor fish in glee,
> with its companions, it takes to the sky, so free!
> In a circle, they dance through the celestial sphere,
> watching carefully for their next prey, clear.

Little Birdie

Little birdie with a voice so fine,
  I wonder, from where do you ever shine?
  Perched high up in that tree.
  Like me, do you also have a dream so free?
  With vocal cords flowing pure gold,
  always melodious, be it warm or cold!
  A gentle invitation, thát pure sweet sound
  I wish to come closer, softly abound!
  What is the theme of your special sweet song?
  Maybe about friends, far and wide, all along?
  Or as you soar over fields so vast,

finding endless joy in food's outcast?
You bring melody to a somber day,
lovely your whistle, pure in every way!
Jingling refrains of love and peace,
bringing joy in every heart's release.

One Day

One day, our oft-spoken word!
    I ever justify myself.
    Reaping fruits from thát shelf!
    One day to others I'll share a tale,
    Today, só busy, don't want to fail!
    One day my time for others to spare,
    now in a hurry with life's every care!
    One day I'll truly enjoy what's in store,
    the good that life has and many more!
    Then I'll turn from my wayward path!
    One day, when all is perfect, free from wrath.
    But the here and now oft forgotten,
    The common 'life-eater' leaves you rotten!

Oh, so subtly, not openly!
An angel of light, this scoundrel to be.
Seducing and holding fast!
Along the reckless path, vision totally overcast!
Perhaps 'one day' you will find the light,
Just as a simple child, this life you'll recite.
But 'one day' may never come to pass!
What then will you do? It's the end, alas!

Victorious
Soul

The sea stretches far and blue,
    so my admiration increases for you!
    For you have toiled, failed, risen again,
    from the depths of the dark ocean's domain!
    Your head held high, a plan you've made,
    endured difficulties on new paths you've laid.
    It was certainly not an easy feat,
    especially in furious waves, full of dread to meet!
    Yet you pressed on and persevered,
    when sea-storms even darkly appeared!

I doff my hat, admire your might,
the ability to fight, push through, day and night!
A salute in prayer shall rise for you,
victorious soul, may you stand firm and true!

Climb the Mountain

Climb the mountain where you stand,
    each step cautiously forward, there to land.
    Keep your eyes turned aloft,
    high where circling birds soar soft.
    Climb foot by foot, slowly but sure,
    to where the highest peaks stretch against heavenly azure.
    If you grow weary, struggling, against rock and slope,
    push on, although frightened, don't give up hope!
    Deepen your courage, move higher, up the mountain's face,
    with feet carefully forward, not ceasing your pace.
    For amidst the heights in the thickest mist,
    lie secrets and wondrous not to be missed.
    The tough climb will be forgot,
    if you continue with brave and steadfast thought.
    Climb the mountain given to you,
    on the other side lies a sea, crystal-clear, new.

When after toil and sorrow you'll see,
    the climb is not in vain, clearly can be.
    Life's very summit, where all looks anew,
    at the top of the mountain, your journey is through!

Close to You

Your nearness is so needed
    to illuminate my life!
    There may be unknown days that wait,
    possible shady dark fate!
    To enfold my mortal being
    with choices, unseeing.
    Your faithful love so divine
    ability and strength, a Heavenly sign!
    Emmanuel in my life
    make this my pursuit and strife.
    When You are near and in control
    guarded from wickedness, my soul!
    Despair, and insecurity recede
    only in Your closeness, where You lead!

Your Will

Just as it is Your will, dear Lord,
      I lay my life before You, outpoured.
      My unformed self did enfold,
      even in the womb, You me uphold!
      My heart for the first time beat,
      Your will for my future to complete!
      Only by Your grace, my Lord,
      Your love, my hungry soul restored!
      While living under the fermament's sun,
      Your Word became the only source I'd run.
      Subjected to Your purpose, O God,
      my soul found rest in the earthly plod.
      All of myself to You I surrender,
      not my options but Yours, forever!
      When stumbling on this path of life,
      Your will lifts me up, through the strife!
      To do what Your heart desires,
      change my steps and inspire!
      Your will is mine, I abide in You,
      stripped from pride, Your will to do!

The Seed

Sown, planted, by our Father Lord
    under His watchful eyes, on the earthly court.
    Seed in the ground,
    rainwater sound,
    The sun from above,
    o'er the seedlings with love.
    Ripe the harvest stands in the field,
    the Sower's heart rejoices to yield!
    Yet the destroyer also sown with intent,
    amidst fair plants, his invasive weeds he lent.
    Deep in the heart of the ungerminated seed
    choose to win or to lose, between vitality or weed?
    To strive and push through to the sun's light,
    or to shrink the bushes' fierceness and blight!

Yielding fruit as the good Sower has ordained,
or choose to waste away, in dismay unstained?

Sitting on the big old Porch

Once again on a summer's eve we sit with Ma and Pa
on our big old porch, gathering to laugh and tra la la...
Gazing up at the wondrous starry sky,
until Drowsy Sandman calls us on the fly!
Early evenings, drawing hopscotch lines with chalk,
or play 'Bunny Jumps,' bouncing along, with cheerful talk!
Great fun when with waistband strings we'd spring,
or whir-whir with a large button on a string!
Such delight as Dad try to spin the whirligig,
with mishaps letting us chuckle for that funny trick!
Of course, the spinning top is the center of much delight.
Sometimes on the grass, running with a colorful kite!
And out on the large lawn right before our stoep,
we'd play loudly, calling each other's names with a funny whoop.
At night, right in front of our old porch,
fireflies gathering like a sparkling torch!
Clever little creatures, in awe we watch the sparkling light
magnificently displayed, who found the most, holding not too tight!
These tiny twinkling stars, beautiful to behold
reflecting freedom, flying off to distant towers, stories untold!
On that porch, enjoying jokes, tales from days yore-
Pa's spooky stories of ghosts galore!
Hearing Ma's apprise of molding soap in the big pot filled with lye,
where candles burn bright, next to the old Aga so high.
Tear-shedding, seeking solace from Ma and Pa,
discussing school friends, teachers, and tra-la-la.
Tasting chocolates, and candy sweets
shiny colorful papers around the treats.
Bending, turning them around dry tree branches,

artistically, transformed into little fragile shiny blanches!
Flower pots with nasturtiums, geraniums, and daisies-
and the porch pillars, draped in rambling roses,
'Tis my longing heart that now reposes!
wondering when was the last time I stepped down
from the porch of fond memories, before it faded to drown!
And oh, how I wish I could just once more linger there
joyfully to idle with my dear ones, without any care!

Your Triumph

In Your love and grace there's beauty, Savior, King,
　　Your deeds are just, as You reign over everything!
　　Infinitely great! A cry for what You've done!
　　Your Word and Spirit stand forever strong as one.
　　From nothing, You fashioned the earth and the skies,
　　therefore my soul calls in worship, to You it complies!
　　Thank You for the Master Plan, the Calvary's cross,
　　where You bore my burden, paying such a cost!
　　All my heavy sins, without number they fall.
　　You washed them away with Your blood, freeing all!
　　There's so much love and grace, O Lord so dear,
　　salvation for me, the sinner, time again near!
　　Close by You in my deepest, deepest woe,
　　there's comfort, You know my sorrow's flow!
　　A breath, You gave humanity to live!
　　On the path with joy, our sins You forgive!
　　So my song of praise resounds, O great Lord!
　　You dwell in my heart, forever a triumph, adored!

Silica and Quartz

A grain of sand, colorless, there you lie,
no eye in particular gazes awry.
Not at all attractive, sprawled on the cold land,
yet streams of water round you on the sand.
Smoothly you rest, 'mongst the thousands of stone,
not for show, like many around sown.
Unnoticed, white, with sharp edges clear,
they tread over you, you've yet to appear.
Unaware of your precious worth deep inside,
as pebbles crunch beneath many in stride.
On the earth's crust, you rest, solid as quartz,
in hues that shift, tilting, canting all sorts.
Without any promises that gleam and shine,
you're just part of the rocks, one in a line.
But one day a hand promising comes,
you're sifted and polished, where beauty hums.

Beautiful quartz, crystal clear in your hue,
placed with other shades in their vibrant view!
Silica small, unimportant, a grain,
now a regal sapphire, proud as a chain.
Cut into a gem, with jasper so bright,
desirable today, in another unique light!

Come to the Waters

The urgent invitation, heed the call to start:
Come to the waters, come buy without gold,
no price for this wine and milk, freely told.
For those who are thirsty, for each and for all,
no payment needed, just answer the call!
No currency required for this bread we seek,
hunger satisfied without labor's peak.
The 'good' fills the hungry with richness and grace,
delighting the soul in this bountiful space!
In ears that will listen lies eternal life,
steadfast in grace, amid chaos and strife.
While He may be found, seek after Him,
while He's still near, call on Him, without grim!
Forsake the wrong paths, the way that is vile,
cleanse darkened thoughts, and follow His style!

He can multiply mercy, forgive every sin!
His heart is compassionate for those who begin.
To confess all your wrongs and your sins to lay bare,
and in seeking His mercy, find grace everywhere!
For His thoughts are above what our minds can perceive,
and His ways are higher than we can ever believe!
The Lord in heaven, where love and mercy flow,
still nourishes the earth and helps the seeds grow!
Higher than human thoughts which often decay,
He grants us good seeds that bring food every day!
So is the Word that proceeds from His mouth,
it never returns empty, let's turn away from doubt!
There's joy, exultation, gladness in praise,
on pathways of peace, forever He stays!
Isaiah 55—processed for my heart!

Sparrow

And there you sit, little sparrow, on the long wire,
　　your beady eyes everywhere, full of desire.
　　Giants walk by, lazily basking in sun,
　　while sometimes a lost pet wanders, just for occasional fun.
　　Your little wings flap with joy and delight,
　　for far in the distance, your friends sing in flight.
　　And fleeting in the bright blue sky you soar,
　　chirping together, carefree, over the shore!
　　Quick, full of energy, you and your friends form the V,
　　in the air a pattern wild, free in unity.
　　You rise up high, then dive down low,
　　beneath the green grass, there are crumbs, a row.
　　The Heavenly Father always takes care,
　　providing for sparrows, with food everywhere!
　　And when I look up again, there you rest,
　　with wings all tucked in and your little head pressed.
　　For the late afternoon sun makes you drowsy on flight!
　　You can peacefully snooze and witness the light!

Rose Garden

Let me wander through a rose-filled garden, on a summer's day,
where most beautiful colors await me to come and play!
Reflected in color, my mood ever pale,
broken heart be mended, and no longer fail!
I'll take photos, admire the colors, one by one,
gaze at the bewitching pink roses, in the summer sun.
Early in the morning, searching the deepest red,
where the loveliest blooms their morning dew long shed.
The soul-enchanting floral splendor soon in parade,
a withered rose awakens, in the summer day's shade.
Beholding the shadows of blue, purple, and black,
entangled in a multitude of thoughts, of sorrow's track.

But the rose garden is also where sweet scents enchant,
beautiful memories, over melancholy, again, rant!
Rose garden, with all your captivating colors' might,

I gladly return to you, on a summer's day so bright!

Sunshine After the Storm

Now go outside, and take a lovely stroll,
fresh breaths of air, after a long lull.
Stormy winds and days spent inside,
wind and weather, in raging tide.
This morning, the deep sea, dark and blue,
the sky merging with it, the blue to imbue.
Each breath, new and fresh again,
sunshine radiating, its joy to maintain.
Gone is the heavy, hazy air,
profound change, brings brightness so fair!
Oh how sparkling now, the renewed mood!
Always captivating, in grace's good.
The Father holds all, in His great plan,
in His Hand, wind and weather, and sunshine's span.
So too, come deep thoughts, after the storm!
Bringing appreciation, warmth in sunshine's form.

Encounter

In reverence, I bow before You! -
    Before You, my Father, King, Lord!
    I desire Your touch, Your liberation too!
    When storms rage hefty in my court
    but Your Voice calls audibly to go fort!
    Full of love, in a gentle summons,
    I hear Your whisper in my muddled slums.
    I need You to rightly direct my deepest needs
    bowing before You, getting rid of all the wicked weeds.

There is no better hope, I can testify!
You, the Only One, to give true hope, to sanctify!
Forever to praise and glorify You!
My sins were washed away by Your blood, so true.
Meet me, hear me, Father Lord,
guide me into a new accord.
What Your Heart requires from me
just to draw nearer to your amazing love.
The precious Heart of my Father, to see!
Although You are in the heavens above.
From ages past to times to come,
You remain the great 'I Am' in shadow or sun.
No 'silver-spoon' in Your all-knowing plan,
but You call the lost, the sick, the poor, each fallen man!
Even the rich, so stubborn, without any woe,
Your heart has a perfect way to forgo.
Not to condemn, but Your guiding Word does speak,
a double-edged sword that allows voluntary choice to seek.
Without coercion, You have so much to freely impart,
Your Father's heart, plan of salvation, to every open heart.
His Love is unfathomably great, it never, ever fails!
Garments of guilt washed in His blood, exchanged without veils.
O the Heart of our loving Father, God
to Him alone glory and praise, to be adored!

The Origin of Joy

My joy is bubbling, not from gain,
    no earthly wealth or splendor to attain!
    My joy finds breath from the Lord on high,
    when clouds unpack their cotton-white in the sky.
    My gladness wishes to burst and sing,
    as fields in colors jubilantly bring!

Butterflies and bees that freely fly,
to honor their Father in the sky.
Overwhelmed with joy at mountains' sight,
standing firm, in quiet peace and resting bedight.
Unstoppable joy bubbles and glows,
when starry sky and crescent moon bestows
The lovely light I clearly see!
With succulents amid the earth openly.
Excited, I wish to sing God's praise,
as water masses their journey to amaze!
My gladness comes from children's smiles so dear,
the elders' wisdom that we hold so near.
The wonder of this world with peoples all,
differently speaking, yet answering God's call!

I rejoice when small creatures I behold,
and mighty beasts across the fields unfold!
My joy unstoppable in fetus unformed,
who becomes a perfect baby, transformed!
I repeat my joy in God the great!
Whose creative works give meaning to a desperate state!
(Phil. 4:4) "Rejoice in the Lord always; again I will say, Rejoice!"

Grace, Still There?

Curse, oppression, and hate -
    No better things for you to state?
    Deception, disdain, and lying speech -
    So satisfying that humanity besieges?
    Boasts, scolds, destroy -
    There's so much more you can employ!
    Gossip, wander, laziness -
    Why not invest in eternal richness?
    Fear, neglect, and self-interest -
    No reward, yet better wealth to quest?
    Meddlesome, tainted by dirty gain -
    Seek the kingdom of God, for worth and refrain!
    Tormenting, complaining, and negative -
    While nature rejoices, meaningfully effective!
    Why... hesitating away from God, that's absurd?
    Instead of submission and reading His eternal Word!

The Israelites in their murmuring and moan
forgot God's Grace, how over them He had thrown!
Indescribable, grand in splendor, God's hope stands fast!
Why allow earthly and sinful bravado on you to cast?
Make sure you have accepted Him!
A heart longing for forgiveness, receive grace's hymn!
What do you store in your empty life's barns?
Time flies suddenly! What about the last turns?
Grace is still abundant, available, full of care!
What will you do with your last breath's share?

A Purpose

A tiny, broken, little bread crumb
    fallen down, a small grain, all undone!
    Unconsciously, trampled upon
    brokened, without life's song!
    Crumbled, no longer in sight
    without any meaning left in its plight?
    Splintered, shattered, but still with a goal
    provision for a sparrow's seeking soul!

Taken from Luke 16:21

The Life of Lazarus

While on tables of plenty, food overflowing, piled high on plates,

Sat a poor man on the street, watching the rich man's friends in their states.

The feasters, merry, clad in purple, carried on without a care,

while the destitute man, alone, lay on the ground by the rich man's lair.

Their lives so full of endless pleasure and delight,

not a single one turned a gaze to poor Lazarus' plight!

It matters not if the man suffered or not, their riches were their bliss!

Hungry Lazarus covered in sores, longed for crumbs to fill a screaming emptiness.

The rich man thought life of plenty will go on and on,

while the weary beggar understood much better, though he spoke not a word, just carried on!

But then a time came when the wealthy life did end,

and Lazarus' sores, even the dogs have come to tend.

The poor beggar was carried away by angels, to find his rest,

while the rich man, in the realm of the dead, now in torment, without peace or fest.

How can he comprehend Lazarus now lying peacefully, in Abraham's embrace?

While at the same time he anguishes, begs for water, aware of flames' scorching trace!

There are agonizing pains in the bitter flame!

Can Lazarus not dip the tip, a finger in water, to ease his parched, suffering frame?

But Abraham's response is sharper than a two-edged sword:

Each received according to their life's deeds, no matter the cord!

And the chasm between them is deep and wide,

no return to life, the once rich man cried!

Time and chances were there for both him and Lazarus,

Moses, other Prophets' teachings, did his heart cuss!

The choice to live in pleasure, without God's command,

brought rightful recompense, a destined lot at hand!

The rich man then wished to warn his family,

sending someone from the dead, making them understand and see.

Finally, the words of Father Abraham echoed true:

If they didn't heed Moses and the Prophets, no one from the dead would convince them too!

*From: Matthéüs 26

How Many Times?

Traitor

How oft does a Judas Iscariot arise,
plotting betrayal with deceitful guise?
Like the disciples, he had the chance to learn the Spirit's ways!
Walking Christ's path in those bygone days.
Together they journeyed down life's long road,
choosing to dwell in God's pure abode.
But Judas' heart had grown selfish and cold,
drifted away from the truth he once was told.
Betrayal festered, fueled by pride's fell fire,
at the table, the All-Knowing saw his dark desire!
"Is it I, Rabbi?" Judas asked with guileful dread,
and Jesus replied, "The words you have said."
How many chances did Judas receive!
Just like the others, a new life to conceive!

"Woe to the one who betrays the Son of Man!"
But Judas followed his own wayward plan.
For the final time, they broke bread and poured wine,
"Take, eat, this is my body," the words were divine.
"My blood, shed for many, the new covenant's seal."
Yet Judas, his heart would not to Christ reveal!
Determined, to the priests Judas did go,
accepted thirty pieces of silver in his prideful show.
Sought the chance to betray and deliver!
Resoluted in his choice, his soul to embitter!
The traitor's sign, a kiss on the cheek,
"The one I kiss, him you must seek."
But the day came, the betrayal was severe,
Judas felt remorse, his grave error did fear!
Innocent blood had been shed and rolled,
Judas stood alone then, his heart was sold!
The priests refused to take back the cursed pay.
"See to it yourself," their callous reply that day!
The blood money hastily cast to the ground,
it was too late, no solace found.
The potter's field was bought, a grave for strangers,
Jeremiah's prophecy was fulfilled, amidst all dangers!
Once the traitor walked in God's grace and light,
Judas faced a solitary, bitter plight!
But Judas, then chose his own destructive way,
He died a lonely death, his soul led astray!

War Cry

O Israel, chosen, special, God's own kin!
    O Israel, you've strayed from His command in sin.
    Still the scholars who His Son do deny,
    and those who His warning Word against earthly faith defy!
    O Israel, how many times more must God speak very hard,
    and innocent blood flows, with your soul so marred?
    O Israel, Abraham, Isaac and Jacob's race,-
    how long in the desert have you toiled the past days?
    While God for you wished to freely believe!
    Guided you with cloud, pillar of fire, step by step to live.
    Through the depths of the sea, parched and dry,
    from Pharaoh's idolatrous land, to new path ply.
    Why today are there just a handful to believe,
    who stand in faith, in the Father above conceive?
    How many times more must your children, your beloved,
    be taken away, destroyed, in somber coffins interred?
    Shots fire out, buildings crumble found,
    still your own path, without thought, a riotous sound!
    Cry out, o people of the righteous God, His judgments are at hand!
    Decide quickly, return to Him, choose the right stand!
    There are also the enemy, and other suffering souls,
    women and children in prisons, enormous tolls!
    Your guilt, o Israel is great, do not see yourself flawless.
    Only the Father Himself without blemish, is spotless.
    But faith and prayer, can bitter remorse, war cries, subdue.
    Grace and peace's radiance, completely to renew!
    Our prayers, o Israel, go out to you,
    be still and clothe yourself in God's adornment, making haste to
do!
    For the heathens, the masses filled with hatred!

Let prayers be raised, for the innocent, debated.
People of God, He loathes your lukewarm condition!
The God of Israel, also hears their sincere call and contrition.

Breath Within Me

In humble gratitude, I take a deep gasp.
 Inhaling outdoor air, a precious gift to grasp.
 The rhythmic beat of my heart each day,
 a precious gift from the Father, thankfully I pray.
 The first breathing as a newborn baby,
 too small to realize what life will carry.
 In growing up, living, rich and full,
 accepting duties through the dull.
 But His Holy Spirit, that lives in me,
 gives power and calmness, I am free!
 The breath He freely pours upon me,
 could never disappoint, in life's degree.
 Yes, while the breath is still within,
 I'll praise Him, stay ever mindful from within!
 His creation, His Word, never to be taken for granted,
 in His creed ever to be branded!
 Until the day my breath returns to Him once more,
 to the One who granted it, forevermore!

Reservoir

Oh Reservoir, if only you could speak!
    For years you've stood, patiently bearing,
    water for all the city's folk, complaining.
    Reservoir, your outer walls look worn and cracked!
    Yet within, water bubbles that give life, are stocked.
    The thirsty fill their vessels from your tank.
    Reservoir, in olden days, the windmill topped you up.

Submersible pumps and pipes, from the borehole's fresh supply,
brought sweet, life-giving water, each drop pure and high!
Reservoir, you steadfastly remain there still!
With modern tech, faster flows, solar panels on the hill...
can they not spruce you up, with paint and skill?
If only you could talk, share your stories true,
of all the lives you've nourished, the amazing work you do!
Reservoir, we're grateful for the bounty you pursue.

Dust

Small speck of dust, pulverized, brown,
you're common in all things, both great and small in town.
The earth's surface covered with your coat,
as fierce winds let you drape the air, afloat.
You scurry and blow, to the housewife's dismay,
as she stands with her dusters, trying to sway.
The whole windowsill in a layer is dressed,
wearisome work, never at rest!
The first man as well, from dust was made,
By God, the great Creator with blessings that do not fade.
And all people will return one day, without fail,
to the dust of the eager earth, which will prevail.

The Question Mark?

Round and perched, you stand there bold,
    after each query, throughout the years untold.
    Sometimes the answer is simple and clear,
    but others make one scratch the head, causing fear!
    And the questions grow more as you getting old,
    a sparse response in a tangled matter, much cold.
    The question mark, it wearies the mind,
    when life unexpectedly happens, it's hard to unwind!
    Sleepless nights are oft acquired,
    with the question mark monster, ever-inspired!
    Pursuing and remaining, causing strife,
    this curious symbol, a part of life!

Experience

The children challenged me, I climbed up, trembling, on high!
Together, with the wet steps to the foam rubber mat, who else will try?
My breath raced, I felt confined, for I stood in the air, meters five,
and I looked before me, smooth foam, splashing water, not feeling alive!
Flat on the stomach, clinging to the sponge rubber beneath.
Turning back? Queue packed, exciting children, I bit on my teeth!
The scared auntie soon rushed far and fast down the slide...
at the moment fearful and anxious, not at all joyful inside!
No longer waiting, my panic and fears now must go!
Then suddenly, the carpet underneath my stomach caught the flow!
Jam on bread, clinging to the mat, this slippery thing, what a slide!
It actually became pleasant, so swiftly on this quick glide!
When suddenly I landed, and waddled to the side,
they pulled me by hand again, I completely lost my pride!

Quicker now up the steps by the Wild Coast's super tube's cause.
Before I moved again, loudly cheering without a pause!
Little courage this second time, half flustered, 'this girl', left the fair!
The speedy sponge floated away as if we're leaving the earth there!
Now I enjoyed and laughed, screaming like a little child!
Quite an experience! This water delight brought joy undefiled!

The Utensil Rack

Knives, forks, dessert spoons, tea spoons, cake forks and
    cake scoops, bread knives, whisks, can-openers, butter-knives and
vegetable-peelers in the rack!
    Useful, useless, sharp, dull, bent, all packed,
    to open what's closed, to gently lift, or just laying on a plate.
    Tasks to lighten the kitchen activities without debate!
    The people-utensil rack is also carefully packed by a Strong Hand,
each with a purpose!
    The working ones, the indispensable, the blunted, the lazy, some
without direction or understanding missing their niftiness!
    Sometimes the sharpest cut swiftly, caring not for damage or pain!
    The whisks are there too, to stir up emotions in a strong refrain!
    Uncounted also those who bear the loads they're assigned!
    Cares and worries bends them, without a rooster's cry behind!

Those that open sealed contents, so light may fall.
Humbled in support, to go fetch the broken ones, standing tall!
Those who gently, resiliently, help to ease some pain.
Others even strippers, reckless, brave, in their life's domain!
Each one created by the Father's hand.
To carry out their life's command!
May the cry be exist as an useful instrument
not for strife, hate and judgment, but willing and consistent!

Leaves

Leaves! Were Adam and Eve's clothing of choice
    Leaves! For animals and humans, a dietary voice
    Leaves! A proverb 'through the leaves' we say
    Leaves! As medicine on limbs that ache and sway
    Leaves! On trees, on flowers, on succulents too
    Leaves! Hanging, wafting, falling, rotting its true
    Leaves! In all shapes and sizes, angular and fair
    Leaves! Living or dead, arranged with utmost care
    Leaves! Round, oval, heart-shaped, so many in sight
    Leaves! Small, large, substantial in plant life's light
    Leaves! Provide cool shade, color, fragrance to share
    Leaves! Used for tea, compost, more than we can bear

Leaves! Coveted source for dyes of every hue
    Leaves! Sometimes sweet jams and drinks anew
    Leaves! Fascinating natural necessities
    Leaves! Sheltering both man and beast, in conservatories
    Leaves! Artistic inspiration colorful engages
    Leaves! Created by God, a blessing through all the ages

The Path That Leads

I walk the comfortable, enticing, pleasurable wide road.

So much to do, fun and revelry, heedless with friends, a red carpet bestowed!

The world lies open, who wants to be serious to learn lessons here?

Time rushes by, while partying late into the night, reckless, daring, without respect or fear!

Glasses full and red, tongues rolling in grandiose delusion.

Every day is so pleasant, pursuing life's wealth, socializing profusion!

But a Voice softly spoke into my heart,-

showing the unwary, indifferent life, empty, without purpose not smart!

Then, almost too late, finally, I turned from that wicked wide way!

I joined the Warning One, onto a different road, the narrow way.

He led me gently, gave wisdom, a meaningful track He said!

Promised His power, His presence, I forged ahead!

The path grew sometimes narrower, there's rocks and stones, I stumbled, fell.

But found love, peace, victory, the Holy Spirit to ever dwell!

Unlike the broad road, Someone cares for my deepest need!

Always standing by me to guide me onward to proceed!

At times I must press forward, but it is the Father's hand that holds and lifts me to go on.

The way is exceedingly narrow, the uphill climbs exhaustingly heavy, but He supports me, along life's dawn!

Occasionally I must grasp at a blade or two,

but in the hope lies new strength, with every step I accrue!

For I walk and press on, surely not alone, He goes before, to carry me over the hills.

When ever the highest mountain, and when worry my heart fills:

"This path, Lord, is far too narrow now, how will I get over that dreadful ridge?"

His arms enfold me, through the valley of death, and safely bring me to the other side!

It is there where wondrous loveliness awaits!

Peace, joy, and rest, beyond all one contemplates.

Love in colors of silver and gold, steadfast in faithful embrace!

Life-giving water, clear with pearls and azure grace.-

His indescribable radiance shining forever bright

in the New Land, joyful and pure in sight!

I Give You My Word

My word is my honor
    as my parents taught me long ago!
    Today I'm so glad
    for it still remains with me, a rad!
    Promises must be kept pure
    to build trust in life's brief allure!
    And in that beautiful Book is written
    living Words that drive me, not smitten!
    The Father speaks clearly
    "Heed My Word" -
    Precious truth sets free,
    a sweet, heavenly accord!
    The Father's promises never stumble or fall,
    amid worry, or whatever may befall!
    His Word He will always uphold!
    There in, no bitter regret enrolled.

He is the God of wonders
    His Word is eternal, substantially without blunders!
    What a sacred kiss, and holy embrace
    ** Isaiah 32:9*

The Little Man

Jesus came passing through Jericho.
    A crowd followed, deeply moved, so!
    He, the One with wondrous power
    waited for all who were in Him cower.
    He understood their deepest fear.
    The little man Zacchaeus ran to peer.
    Chief tax collector in the rich man's home,
    smart, making money for that roam.

He too wanted to see Jesus!
To know Him, whom all so revere, His thesis!
There he spotted the fig tree looming,
now he must hurry not to be dooming!
The great crowd came rushing near.
Zacchaeus' climb grew dire, severe!
Sitting, he viewed the tumultuous throng - he shivered!
For suddenly Jesus stood still, the crowd all quivered!
Words spoken so clearly, aimed at him.
He could scarce believe his ears grew not dim!
Was that the Voice of Jesus speaking? he listened, overjoyed:
"Zacchaeus, hurry down, in your home I must be employed!"
The crowd grumbled about this sinful man!
How could the Master stay in his house, their view not grand?
Zacchaeus gratefully explained his case-
fourfold he would repay what he unjustly took,
and half his goods for the poor, he would gladly place!

And Jesus granted salvation to the tax collector and his home

The lost one, now Abraham's son, sought and saved, the seed was sown!

Luke 19:10 "For the Son of Man came to seek and to save the lost."

Converse with the Lord

We discuss all matters, in circles of friends.
Delve into and follow, what trouble portends.
Yet no answer came, we pretend,
not understanding the trend!
So eager, chattering about others' keen sight!
Reluctant to let go of the worldly fright.
The tone is quite lively, but then comes the woe!
Part of the gossip, nothing bars the way.
Grasping at a straw, 'status' calms our sway.
Guilty, strange feelings, calamity that is so!
Soft the Small Voice speaks, yet we more readily heed!
Advice of others, little time do we concede-
to the heavenly stillness, in His presence to be!
Share with Him our burdens, shadows and bitter falls.
He waits with open arms for our approach to His calls!
To speak with our Lord, the right path to attain.
Jesus the One who will always sustain,-
His wondrous working power in our lives will prevail!
Rather talk to Him, His answer will not fail!

Weep Before the Lord

Lord, today I weep before You
    over suffering, heartaches, my thoughts are askew.
    life's losses that I cannot understand!
    There's bitter pain and fear all around the land!
    The robbed, the murdered, the beaten down
    Children and the aged without a caregiver's gown
    Those in homes and prisons, mostly downtrodden.
    so many lies begging in the mud, left forgotten!
    Lord, my heart so aching, I cry before You
    for those without food or clothes, in this world so cruel.
    And for the war-cries when bombs come raining down!
    Displaced, to foreign lands, without grace to rule.
    I seek solace, Father, Lord
    and Your Word for the others' despair!
    For those addicted, drunk, in self-destruction abhorred
    give them clear eyes, to understand the course.

I shall not murmur,
but seek answers in the Bible's way
when temptations come to deter Your goodness,
lest it in haze I betray!

The Broken Bread

From heaven it shall descend -
    a true tale to comprehend!
    God's Bread, He is the One,
    through Him His power has ever won!
    Life to the world it will mean,
    for those who in Him shall lean!
    He, Jesus, the bread of eternal life,
    only He has seen the Father, as is rife.
    To still the hunger and thirst of man -
    this Bread, as per God's design and plan!
    And Jesus knew the bread to break,
    His own body, crushed to shred.
    A supper, for mankind's sake -
    He was scorned, His body to break!
    Sorrows and separation, not so great,
    broken Bread for our guilt, our state!

Pierced for our transgressions' sake,
shattered and slain, our ransom to make!
Our iniquities and wounds were smashed on Him.
He was crushed so that peace and healing could ever win!
To turn wandering sheep from their own destructive sway -
back to Him, the Lamb, silently on to the narrow way!
The Bread was broken to bear our sin,
poured out in death, só victoriously to win!

Moses on Mount Sinai

Three months after the exodus from Egypt,
    there were murmurs among the people's script.
    In Sinai, they set up camp right across the mountain
    where they would later provoke God and disountin'
    And Moses climbed up, for he heard the Voice-
    God's given Message to discipline the people's choice.
    For their sake, the Egyptians were overthrown
    on eagle's wings, Israel was carried and brought here alone!
    But they must listen and keep His covenant
    the whole earth His, holding a steadfast, governant!
    The elders were summoned - God sought a Holy nation.
    It was here where Moses learned under the sacred cloud's station.
    The people's unanimous decision related to God.
    They have agreed on this remarkable lot.
    Purified themselves, led them up the mountain the third day
    God will descend on Mount Sinai, to say!

A boundary line must be set where none might touch,
    not even a foot against the Holy Mountain, in a clutch.
    It was the third day, there were crashes of thunder, a thick cloud!
    Trumpets sounded, people trembled, on the mountain smoke
billowed!
    The Lord descended in fire at the peak
    at the foot of Sinai, Israel wandered, waiting for God to speak.
    The mountain quaked heavily, God's voice to Moses came:
    "Up to the top of the mountain, Moses," there's smoke, a flame!
    The people were afraid to die, they wished Moses would speak
quickly and clear

but he did convey: "Do not sin and no fear!"

God came to test, so reverence must appear!

Moses then went up, near the 'dark clouds,' to God.

He waited for His command, about Israel's lot.

Two tablets of the Testimony were given to Moses,

of stone inscribed with the finger of God, written in process!

Moses was forty days and forty nights on the mountain.

Doubt reigned, a golden calf was built, they started pountin'

Even Aaron built an altar, they danced before this idol

God observed the unbelief, the sinful breeding nidal!

Moses pleaded for grace, prevented God's sharp blade, a sheath,-

for God had revealed the people's malicious deeds underneath!

Moses' anger flared over the lawlessness when he saw the calf.

The stone tablets were shattered, Moses prayed for restoration, no easy path!

With new stone tablets, Moses climbed up again, willingly

God's grace was so great, He spoke with Moses as a friend, sincerely!

proses - The plural of "prose," referring to written or spoken language in its ordinary form, without metrical structure.

Winged Creatures

Birds of every feather fair,
    created by the Lord with care.
    Adorned in colors rich and bright,
    like humans in their endless plight.
    Both clean and unclean, God decrees what to eat,
    but stubborn man in sorrow's grasp to meet,
    Many birds deprived, ensnared and bound,
    or caged in falsehood, without faith profound.
    Yet God knows each bird upon the mountain crest,
    and all His children, His own, life's test.
    The birds of Heaven raise their songs of praise,
    amid the branches, love's sweet music plays.
    Up there, the winged ones, from whom man can learn
    to joyfully their Maker's glory ever sing!
    With young doves' blood, for cleansing duly offered,
    by priests made pure, the old laws ordered.

But Jesus came, the highest price to pay,
    His blood washed all unrighteousness away.
    Weed freely sow, birds eagerly pluck them from the ground,
    the same to those misled, on darkened paths that bound.
    And sometimes in his pride and vain conceit,
    man forgets God who bears their children sweet.
    As a mother swan, bearing her child, history's proof is clear:
    Trust in the Lord, He will not disappoint, He's always near!
    Manna, meat, for food, like sand by the sea,
    people walking in joy, blessed by the Lord's decree.
    But when abominations with care did increase,

they forgot God, no longer praying for peace.
The birds of Heaven fly away to sing elsewhere.
The Holy Spirit departs, without human repent and care.
The chief baker's dream, interpreted by Joseph, who believed,
birds from the basket on his head, Pharaoh's death, he perceived.

God made man little lower than the divine,
so he has reason to magnify the Name sublime!
As birds of Heaven glorify their Maker true,
He longs for songs of praise, man's hearts, anew!

Sunflower Being

Thunderclouds, deeply hidden behind the azure sphere.
    Sunlight now richly colors the Sunflower's face here.
    Dancing and singing in the bright sunshine,
    facing the rays, exultingly, intertwine!
    Oh, it's delightful to dance, to sway, the day to glide,
    with steadfast courage, the sweetest joys of life to abide.
    After gloomy storm-filled days, applauding, praising to sing!
    In sunny attire, honor unto the Creator to bring!

O Sunflower, yellow, gold, and full of fairest hue,
    firm and spontaneous, you stand there to view.
    Mostly strong and radiant, so in your special place,
    where the sun's delight breaks through, with joy in your face.
    Blossoming in the creation of the Supreme Being,
    sparkling, rejoicing, Sunflower's heart's praising!

Closed Doors

Are the doors closing in on you,
    stumbling along to pursue?
    With a raging world around, cold, without care?
    Is it not time, your heart to openly share?
    For He is the One ever to be watchful,
    He understands grief, sorrows and is truthful.
    Humbly bow down on your knees before Him,
    in deep acknowledgment of guilt and sin.
    Speak, tell Him what deeply scars your heart,
    all the concerns in your human part.
    He, the One who knows just what you mean,
    when childlike at His feet, a cool solace was seen!
    He'll open greater doors for you,
    so that in peace you ever may walk through!
    Not what you have in mind or self achieved,
    rather His leading, to Him to cleave.
    And when you cry out in winter's cold,
    His love, His care will miraculously unfold!
    Forever covered in His caring love,
    what a glorious solemn troth!

Day to Day

In the rising and in the going to bed,
    maybe eight hours apart, that's what's said. -
    How early the rising, how late the 'night' has led?
    But in between, in that specific day,
    programmed with many tasks that sway!
    For a visit sometimes only a while,
    and just a little bit of joy and style.
    Then comes the night with a sweet dream,
    a snore or two for others who they deem.
    Or maybe a nightmare about tomorrow's task,
    challenges can sometimes be overwhelming to ask!

Noctambulism

In deep slumber, it is done,
the psyche disturbed, not at one.
Wide-open eyes, in the hallway's span,
too much wine or even medicine, too strong a plan.
Or something in the genes, or lack of sleep gone.
Then half-awake, yet sleeping, to rise anon.
Without awareness, like a deceiving sheep,
slumbering, wandering in the midnight's keep.
Consciousness vanishes in the midnight's hour,
dangerous for this motion to overpower.
Walk, sleep, even eat, a motorized pace,
may be confusing, causing others the wanderer to trace!
Better not to wake her up, rather softly back to bed,
equally at rest instead!
Noctambulism - Sleepwalking - Wandering in one's sleep.

Don't miss out!

Visit the website below and you can sign up to receive emails whenever Johanita Viljoen publishes a new book. There's no charge and no obligation.

https://books2read.com/r/B-A-DWMVC-LAPIF

BOOKS2READ

Connecting independent readers to independent writers.

About the Author

KJV Psalms 104:24 O Lord, how manifold are thy works!

I don't think it's necessary for more descriptive words concerning the why or the whom of these poems from my heart. My joy overflows with thankfulness and humbleness. I desire to reach out to a world unreachable, lost, and lonely with dancing lyrics on my tongue. The message is pure: There is always hope in Jesus Christ!

Thanks for your positive support.

Read more at https://www.facebook.com/JohanitaSongPoem.

About the Publisher

Always looking for new ideas and getting it out there!
Readers are number one!
Read more at https://www.facebook.com/JohanitaSongPoem.

9 798230 529583